FREE MASK

You Will Need:

- Thin elastic, wool or string

- Scissors

- Sticky Tape

Instructions:

1. Pull out the mask page.
2. Pop out the mask.
3. Cut enough elastic/wool/string to fit around the back of your head.
4. Attach to the back of the mask with some sticky tape.
5. Have fun with your new mask!

SCISSORS ARE SHARP! ASK AN ADULT FOR HELP BEFORE USING.

Contents

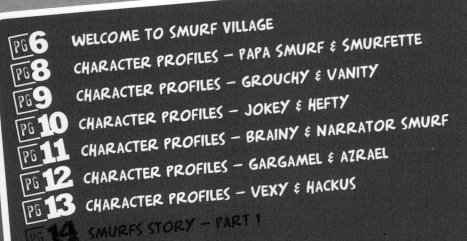

Pedigree®
PUBLISHED 2013.

PEDIGREE BOOKS LIMITED. BEECH HILL HOUSE.
WALNUT GARDENS. EXETER. DEVON EX4 4DH
WWW.PEDIGREEBOOKS.COM
BOOKS@PEDIGREEGROUP.CO.UK

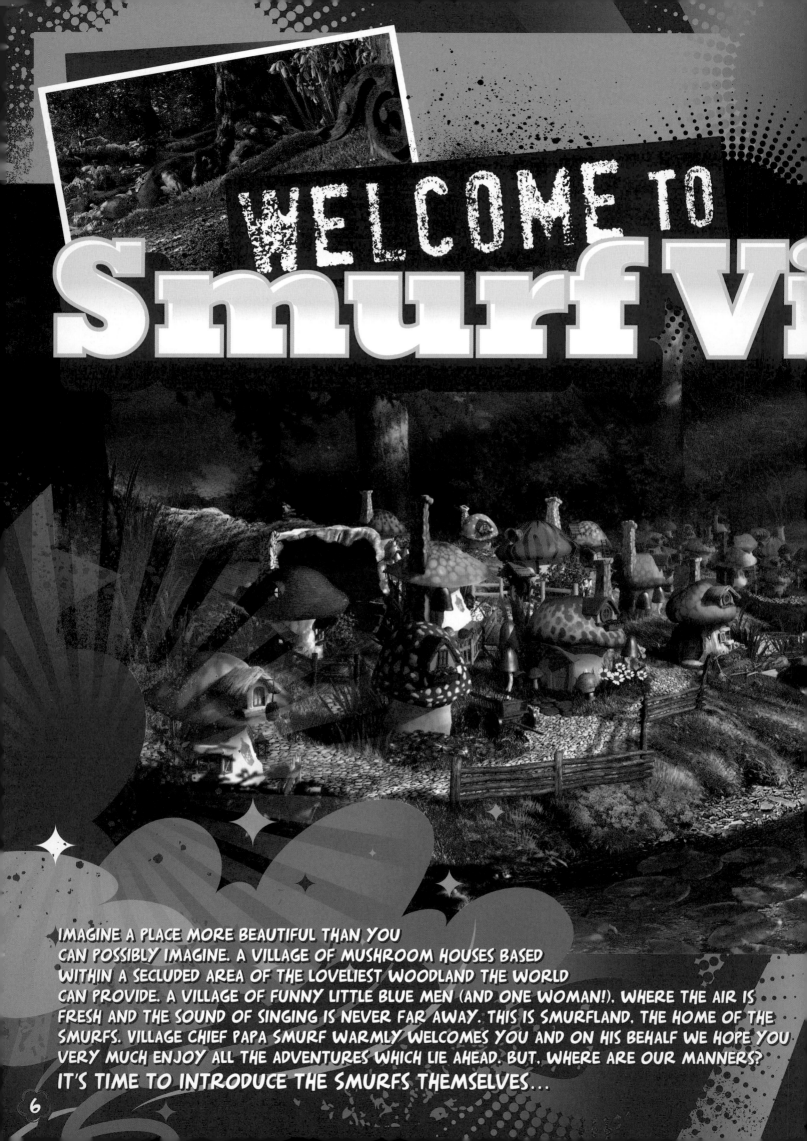

WELCOME TO Smurf Vi

IMAGINE A PLACE MORE BEAUTIFUL THAN YOU
CAN POSSIBLY IMAGINE. A VILLAGE OF MUSHROOM HOUSES BASED
WITHIN A SECLUDED AREA OF THE LOVELIEST WOODLAND THE WORLD
CAN PROVIDE. A VILLAGE OF FUNNY LITTLE BLUE MEN (AND ONE WOMAN!). WHERE THE AIR IS
FRESH AND THE SOUND OF SINGING IS NEVER FAR AWAY. THIS IS SMURFLAND. THE HOME OF THE
SMURFS. VILLAGE CHIEF PAPA SMURF WARMLY WELCOMES YOU AND ON HIS BEHALF WE HOPE YOU
VERY MUCH ENJOY ALL THE ADVENTURES WHICH LIE AHEAD. BUT. WHERE ARE OUR MANNERS?
IT'S TIME TO INTRODUCE THE SMURFS THEMSELVES...

6

llage

© Peyo 7

Papa Smurf

JOB TITLE: VILLAGE CHIEF.

DISTINGUISHING FEATURES: RED OUTFIT AND WHITE BEARD. AT OVER 500 YEARS OLD. PAPA IS BY FAR THE OLDEST OF THE SMURFS. HE IS OCCASIONALLY MISTAKEN FOR A SMURF FATHER CHRISTMAS.

HOBBIES: COLLECTING POTIONS AND CREATING MAGICAL FORMULAS DESIGNED TO PROTECT THE OTHER SMURFS FROM GARGAMEL.

MOST LIKELY TO BE FOUND: REASSURING THE OTHER SMURFS WITH HIS WORDS OF GUIDANCE AND WISDOM.

LEAST LIKELY TO BE FOUND: DASHING AROUND IN A PANIC.

JOB TITLE: THE ONLY GIRL SMURF IN THE VILLAGE.

DISTINGUISHING FEATURES: GOOD LOOKS. BLONDE HAIR.

HOBBIES: WANDERING BY THE LAKE OR RIDING ON THE BACK OF A BIRD. BUT PERHAPS OCCASIONALLY WORRYING ABOUT HER ORIGINS AS THE CREATION OF GARGAMEL.

MOST LIKELY TO BE FOUND: LEADING A CHORUS OF THE SMURFING SONG.

LEAST LIKELY TO BE FOUND: LOSING HER TEMPER WITH HER FELLOW SMURFS.

FACT FILE:

Smurfette

Grouchy

FACT FILE:

JOB TITLE:
VILLAGE GRUMPYPANTS.

DISTINGUISHING FEATURES:
GRUMPINESS. GLOOMY NEGATIVE
OUTLOOK. BUT DEEP DOWN.
ACTUALLY VERY NICE.

HOBBIES: MOANING. POINTING
OUT THE FLAWS IN ANY PLAN.
LOOKING ON THE DOWNSIDE.
AT LEAST. AT FIRST. LATER HE HAS
A SUDDEN CHANGE OF ATTITUDE...

MOST LIKELY TO BE FOUND:
FROWNING.

LEAST LIKELY TO BE FOUND:
SAYING: "CHEER UP EVERYONE!
THINGS CAN ONLY GET BETTER!
LET'S HAVE A SINGSONG!"

Vanity

FACT FILE:

JOB TITLE: THE FAIREST SMURF
OF ALL?

DISTINGUISHING FEATURES:
NEVER WITHOUT A MIRROR.
VANITY HAS ONE DEEP AND GENUINE
LOVE...HIMSELF.

HOBBIES: GAZING LOVINGLY AT HIS
OWN REFLECTION.

MOST LIKELY TO BE FOUND:
IN FRONT OF A MIRROR.
PERFECTING HIS APPEARANCE.

LEAST LIKELY TO BE FOUND:
IN A RUFFLED. UNTIDY STATE.
HAVING JUST GOT OUT OF BED.

Jokey

JOB TITLE: VILLAGE COMEDIAN.

DISTINGUISHING FEATURES:
ALWAYS SMILING AND OFTEN WITH A
PRESENT IN HIS HANDS.

HOBBIES: PLOTTING A PRACTICAL
JOKE: OFTEN IN THE FORM OF AN
EXPLODING GIFT.

MOST LIKELY TO BE FOUND:
LAUGHING.

LEAST LIKELY TO BE FOUND:
HANGING AROUND WITH GROUCHY.
THE TWO HAVE LITTLE IN COMMON.

FACT FILE:

MEET THE SMU

JOB TITLE: SPORTY SMURF.

DISTINGUISHING FEATURES:
STRENGTH AND SPORTINESS.

HOBBIES: NAME A SPORT! CHANCES
ARE. HEFTY HAS MASTERED IT.

MOST LIKELY TO BE FOUND:
LIFTING WEIGHTS OR
DEMONSTRATING SOME OTHER
INCREDIBLE FEAT OF STRENGTH.

LEAST LIKELY TO BE FOUND:
READING POETRY. COLLECTING
STAMPS OR FLOWER ARRANGING.

FACT FILE:

Hefty

© Peyo

Brainy

FACT FILE:

JOB TITLE: VILLAGE BRAINBOX.

DISTINGUISHING FEATURES: GLASSES. EXTREME INTELLIGENCE.

HOBBIES: SHOWING OFF. POINTING OUT ANOTHER SMURF'S MISTAKES. TAKING LIFE A BIT TOO SERIOUSLY.

MOST LIKELY TO BE FOUND: READING. MAKING HIMSELF MORE CLEVER.

LEAST LIKELY TO BE FOUND: ROLLING AROUND IDLY IN THE GRASS. RELAXING.

JOB TITLE: SMURF STORYTELLER.

DISTINGUISHING FEATURES: NARRATOR SMURF HAS A BIZARRE TENDENCY TO CONSTANTLY DESCRIBE EVERYTHING THAT'S HAPPENING AS IT HAPPENS.

HOBBIES: ANNOYING THE OTHER SMURFS BY NARRATING ON EVERYTHING.

MOST LIKELY TO BE FOUND: READING TO THE AUDIENCE AT THE BEGINNING AND END OF A FILM.

LEAST LIKELY TO BE FOUND: GIVING HIS VOICE A WELL EARNED REST.

FACT FILE:

Narrator Smurf

Gargamel

FACT FILE:

JOB TITLE: GLOBAL SUPERVILLAIN/SORCERER/STAR OF THE STAGE/ GARGAMEL LE GREAT.

DISTINGUISHING FEATURES: HIDEOUS APPEARANCE AND ALMOST PERMANENT BAD TEMPER. EVIL. OBSESSED WITH SMURFS. ALWAYS ACCOMPANIED BY AZRAEL.

HOBBIES: STRUGGLING TO TAKE OVER THE WORLD. PERFORMING HIS POPULAR MAGIC SHOW IN FRONT OF HUGE AUDIENCES. ATTEMPTING HYPNOSIS. FORCING HIS AUDIENCES TO BOW TO HIM. BY USING MAGIC.

MOST LIKELY TO BE FOUND: IN HIS LABORATORY. INTENT ON FINDING SOME WAY TO EXTRACT MORE ESSENCE FROM THE SMURFS. THUS ENABLING HIM TO TAKE OVER THE WORLD.

LEAST LIKELY TO BE FOUND: HELPING AN OLD LADY ACROSS THE ROAD. GIVING MONEY TO CHARITY. BEING NICE.

FACT FILE:

JOB TITLE: GARGAMEL'S CAT.

DISTINGUISHING FEATURES: THE USUAL CAT FEATURES: WHISKERS AND TAIL EXCEPT OCCASIONALLY AZRAEL HAS HIS FELINE BODY INCREASED TO COLOSSAL SIZE BY HIS MASTER'S MAGIC.

HOBBIES: ATTEMPTING TO COMMUNICATE WITH GARGAMEL PURELY BY MEOWING.

MOST LIKELY TO BE FOUND: BEING TORMENTED BY THE NAUGHTIES OR BEING CHUCKED OUT OF GARGAMEL'S CARRIAGE.

LEAST LIKELY TO BE FOUND: TAKING A SWIM.

Azrael

Vexy

FACT FILE:

JOB TITLE: NAUGHTIE.

DISTINGUISHING FEATURES:
VERY MUCH NAUGHTY BY NATURE.
AT LEAST SO SHE THINKS UNTIL ONE
DAY SHE MEETS A CERTAIN SMURF
CALLED SMURFETTE...

HOBBIES: KIDNAPPING SMURFETTE.
CAUSING MAYHEM. TRYING TO
PLEASE HER "FATHER" GARGAMEL.

MOST LIKELY TO BE FOUND:
TAKING A RIDE ON A STORK OR
RACING DOWN THE STREETS OF
PARIS IN A TROLLEY.

LEAST LIKELY TO BE FOUND:
IN BALLET CLASS.

MEET THE NAUGHTIES

JOB TITLE: NAUGHTIE.

DISTINGUISHING FEATURES:
WILD. MORE LIKE AN UNTAMED
BEAST THAN ANYTHING ELSE.

HOBBIES: SAYING HIS OWN NAME
"HACKUS" REPEATEDLY.

MOST LIKELY TO BE FOUND:
COOKING UP A STORM OF TROUBLE
IN A FRENCH SWEETSHOP.

LEAST LIKELY TO BE FOUND:
DELIVERING A TWO HOUR LECTURE
ON STAGE AT THE PARIS
OPERA HOUSE.

FACT FILE:

Hackus

13

Smurfet

has an unhappy birthd

SMUR

ALL WAS WELL IN SMURF VILLAGE.
WELL ALMOST ALL....

For not everyone in the Village was happy.
In her sleep, Smurfette was having a bad dream.

In her dream, she remembered how she had first been created by the evil Gargamel, the power hungry sorcerer who had been intent on wreaking havoc amongst the Smurfs. But she also remembered, more happily, how Papa Smurf had then made her into Smurfette, the darling of the Smurf Village using a combination of kindness, love, delicious fruit pies and a secret magical formula. It was a happy memory, the memory of her rebirth. But then the dream grew more unsettled…

She saw herself transformed into a menacing figure terrorising the other Smurfs as Gargamel – her father in the dream – looked on approvingly and laughing…

Smurfette woke with a start. What a nightmare! Thankfully Papa Smurf heard her cry out in her sleep and was already by her side.

"There, there" the old Smurf said, hugging her. "Were you having that nightmare again?"

Smurfette choked back her tears. "Every year, the night before my birthday, I have these horrible dreams and they remind me how different I am."

"OH DEAR," PAPA SIGHED. "IT DOESN'T MATTER WHERE YOU CAME FROM. WHAT MATTERS IS WHO YOU CHOOSE TO BE."

© Peyo

Indeed, at that very moment, unknown to her, the Village was busy with preparations for Smurfette's surprise birthday party.

Just then, the door to Smurfette's Mushroom began to open. "She's coming!" shouted Panicky. The Smurfs flew into a scramble hiding everything from sight.
Nobody wanted Smurfette's surprise to be spoiled.

Amazingly, by the time Smurfette came out, everything – cakes, decorations and all – had been hidden from sight.

"Hey guys," said Smurfette innocently. "Anyone want to go to the meadow with me?"
But nobody did. In truth, the other Smurfs secretly wanted her to leave simply because they wanted to continue setting things up for her own secret party. Saddened, Smurfette dropped her head and walked gloomily towards the forest.

"Nobody seems to want me here," she mused. "I wonder where I belong?"

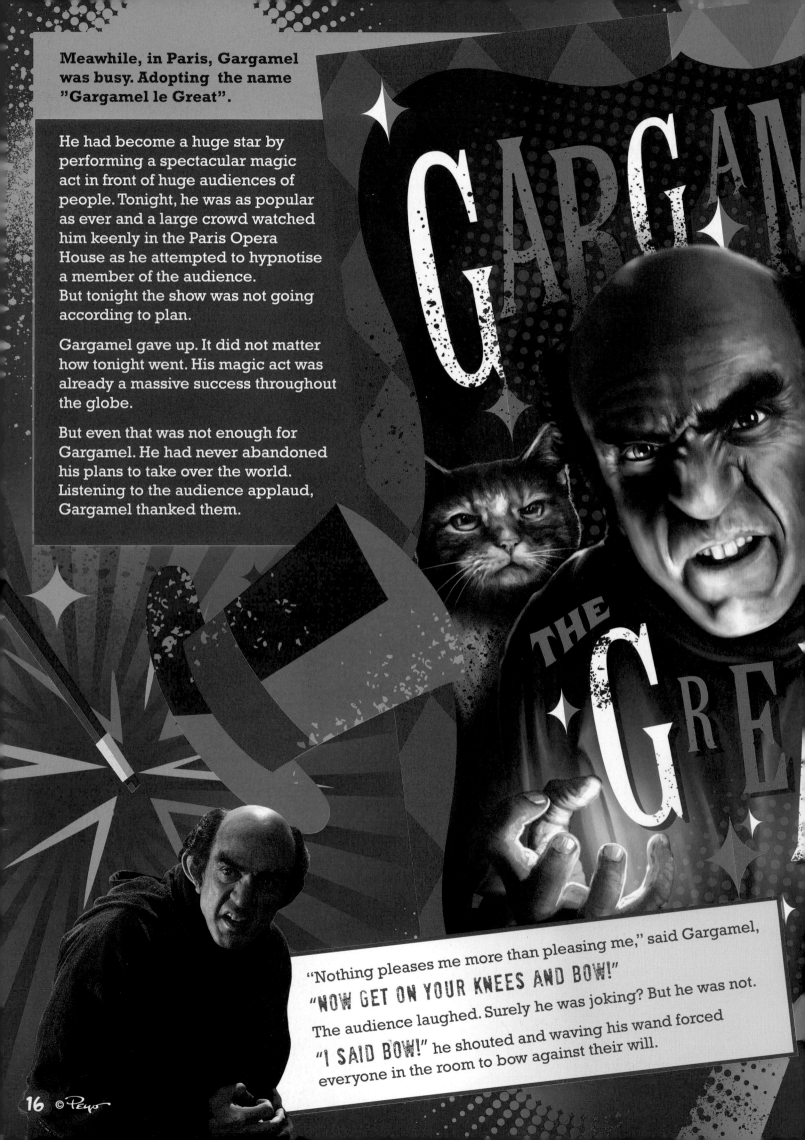

Meawhile, in Paris, Gargamel was busy. Adopting the name "Gargamel le Great".

He had become a huge star by performing a spectacular magic act in front of huge audiences of people. Tonight, he was as popular as ever and a large crowd watched him keenly in the Paris Opera House as he attempted to hypnotise a member of the audience.
But tonight the show was not going according to plan.

Gargamel gave up. It did not matter how tonight went. His magic act was already a massive success throughout the globe.

But even that was not enough for Gargamel. He had never abandoned his plans to take over the world. Listening to the audience applaud, Gargamel thanked them.

"Nothing pleases me more than pleasing me," said Gargamel, "NOW GET ON YOUR KNEES AND BOW!" The audience laughed. Surely he was joking? But he was not. "I SAID BOW!" he shouted and waving his wand forced everyone in the room to bow against their will.

© Peyo

Afterwards, in Gargamel's luxury carriage, Gargamel's cat Azrael meowed at him. The cat didn't approve of its owner's behaviour. By making the audience bow, Gargamel had wasted some of the valuable essence he had extracted from Papa Smurf in New York. And supplies were running low. Fortunately for him, Gargamel had a plan. And he had just enough essence left to achieve it.

Back at his hotel, Gargamel discovered a box. What could it be? "Ooh look! A present!" Gargamel said excitedly. But he soon noticed the name written on the box. "Oh! Azrael. It's for you."

Azrael looked into the box warily. Gargamel watched impatiently. "Don't be such a scaredy cat!" he urged. "It's not a trap. It's a gift. Partake!"

Cautiously, Azrael opened the box. But...what was this? The box appeared to be empty. Empty that is...except for a red dot.

Suddenly, the dot jumped out of the box. Azrael leapt on it and chased it around the room until, it suddenly changed into a short little girl with dark hair. Like a Smurf, only paler.

"Hello, Kitty!" said the creature. "I'm Vexy!" Another creature, Hackus, much wilder, had appeared on the other side of the room aswell.

"Hackus! Hackus! Hackus!" was all he said.

Azrael did not like the newcomers one bit but Gargamel was clearly happy to see them. "Very amusing my little Naughties!"

"Do we please you, Father?" asked Vexy. Now the mad wizard looked less happy.

"No, you don't. You know what would please me?

If your putrid pale essence could endow me with real magic like that of a true blue Smurf. That would excite me. Instead, you're just deeply disappointing experiment.

ESSENCE DE
Smurf

Bring me my plan, Azrael!" Azrael produced a tablet. "This isn't my writing parchment!" said Gargamel. Still, he touched the screen which brought up an image of the Smurfs' village. But it wasn't as it should be: the tablet showed an image of the village in a terrible state. It was a smoking ruin.

Gargamel pointed at the screen: "This is our aim. Total destruction of Smurf Village!" Gargamel was so happy at the thought of this that he started to cry. "I'm sorry. I always get emotional at this part".

Gargamel pressed another button and a picture of the Eiffel Tower in Paris came up. "The very reason we chose Paris was for this great iron antennae. It's the only way to harness enough energy to create a portal right into Smurf Village."

Suddenly he noticed something. Vexy and Hackus were very pale and weak. Realising the two were hungry he poured some essence into their mouths saving the last drop to put into his new Dragon Wand.

"Now. To the antennae!" the mad wizard cried.

Later, outside the Eiffel Tower, Gargamel used his wand to create a whirlpool in the nearby River Seine. "Perfect! Just enough essence to open the portal!" the sorcerer said.

However, there was a problem. When Gargamel tried to leap into the portal he got stuck! The portal was much too small. He spun around as if he was in a washing machine.

Vexy saw her chance. "Father, I can fit through there."

Gargamel agreed: "Now I must warn you, your destination is a horror. It ruined your sister Smurfette. That ridiculous little Papa Smurf brainwashed her and turned against me! She's a traitor! But she's the one who knows the formula.

Now, go and get her!" Picking Vexy up, he aimed her like a dart and flung her into the portal.

19

In Smurf Village, a gloomy Smurfette was walking along the bank of the pond.

"I can't believe they didn't remember my birthday." She looked thoughtfully into her own reflection in the river. "It's because I'm not one of them".

But her sadness soon turned into horror as the image of Vexy suddenly rose out of her reflection! Smurfette began to run away but Vexy spoke:

"PLEASE HELP! I ESCAPED...FROM THE EVIL WIZARD WHO MADE ME."

Smurfette was baffled. "Do you mean Gargamel? He made you? But that means ...you're just like me!"

Smurfette rushed to her but Vexy suddenly grabbed her. Vexy dragged the screaming Smurfette towards the river. "Father's going to be very happy!" said Vexy.

The Smurfs had almost finished preparing the party when they heard Smurfette's screams for help. "Smurfette's in trouble!" said Handy. The Smurfs rushed to help and arrived just in time to see her being dragged into the portal.

"She's being Smurfnapped!" said Greedy

Vexy smiled wickedly, pushed Smurfette into the portal and then jumped in herself.

"So long!" she said. The portal closed before the other Smurfs could reach it.

Brainy thought hard. "It doesn't take a genius to tell you, but I will anyway: this is the work of Gargamel!"

21

PAPA'S Paris Puzzler

PAPA SMURF IS HOPELESSLY LOST IN PARIS. CAN YOU HELP HIM FIND AS MANY OTHER CHARACTERS IN THIS WORDSEARCH AS POSSIBLE? SOME PARIS LANDMARKS HAVE ALSO BEEN THROWN IN TO HELP PAPA GET HIS BEARINGS. WORDS (LISTED BELOW) MAY APPEAR GOING UPWARDS, DOWNWARDS, LONGWAYS AND BACKWARDS. BUT WATCH OUT! ONE OF THE LISTED WORDS ISN'T INCLUDED IN THE GRID. CAN YOU SPOT WHICH ONE?

BLUE · BRAINY · CLUMSY · EIFFEL TOWER
GRACE · GROUCHY · SMURFETTE · PATRICK
RIVER SEINE · VANITY · VICTOR

```
C R D O L K M X O S F R S J A A C L U M J I O E
J G C P C C R B U I R Z A N L M O N S Y P O P I
A A B O L L P O N T I E N O O P K L D A P O S F
W R B L U E W E P O V I P O P A B O M K O P M F
S G R A M I P K S W E G R A C E H A N D O I U E
T A A S S F R E Y E R T Y R O S T T H U N K R L
O F G M Y G P O H P S O P O O P K R D A P O S T
W S H L H A N N C G E J I O E P E O S C I I M O
R C O L L E G P U N I L L I O P A T B S A P X W
E H O N O E S T O D N B O G O B I C E L K P G E
V I T I N Y S P R K E L J M I R A I L E S I J R
E N E R R Y E T G P O P Y T I N A V J U L H S O
S M U R F E T T E I A N O K I L L G R E R A L
Y E L O Y Y J U D A P O M I O M J O H W K R O U
S A R T E F R E W C R R F U K I I L B R A I N Y
```

HAVE YOU FOUND ALL THE WORDS?

ANSWERS ON PAGE 77

22 © Peyo

HELP SMURFETTE ESCAPE!

HELP!.

SMURFETTE HAS BEEN KIDNAPPED BY THE NAUGHTIES AND TAKEN TO GARGAMEL'S LAIR.

BUT FEAR NOT! THERE IS AN ESCAPE ROUTE. IN FACT. THERE ARE THREE.

CAN YOU HELP SMURFETTE AVOID THE TWO PATHS WHICH WILL LEAD HER TO VEXY AND HACKUS AND HELP HER FIND THE ROUTE TO PAPA SMURF AND SAFETY?

GOOD LUCK!

ANSWER ON PAGE 77

23

Brainy's
CHALLENGE

HAVE FUN!

1 AT THE START OF THE STORY, THE SMURFS ARE PLANNING A CELEBRATION. WHY?

- A It's Smurfette's birthday party.
- B Hefty has just won an important running race.
- C The Smurfs have decided to visit Patrick and Grace.

2 WHO KIDNAPS SMURFETTE?

- A Gargamel.
- B The Naughties, Vexy and Hackus.
- C Azrael.

3 SMURFETTE HAS A BAD DREAM AT THE START OF THE STORY. WHAT CAUSES IT?

- A She is scared of Gargamel.
- B She is worried that she may grow up to be like Gargamel.
- C She ate too much Smurf cheese the night before.

4 GARGAMEL HAS BECOME FAMOUS SINCE THE LAST SMURF ADVENTURE. WHY?

- A He has become a famous puppet expert.
- B He hosts his own TV show "Good Morning with Gargamel."
- C He is host of a famous magic show which tours the world.

5 WHICH OF THESE HAPPENS TO GROUCHY DURING THE STORY?

- A He decides to be less grumpy and more positive.
- B He learns to speak French.
- C He rides on the back of a bird.

6 VICTOR GETS TURNED INTO WHICH CREATURE?

- A A stork.
- B A giant cat.
- C A duck.

© Peyo

THINK YOU KNOW EVERYTHING THERE IS TO KNOW ABOUT THE SMURFS AND THEIR LATEST ADVENTURES?

7 WHO IS VICTOR?

A Patrick's uncle.

B Patrick's step-father.

C Patrick's boss.

8 WHICH CITY DO THE SMURFS TRAVEL TO IN THIS STORY?

A London.

B New York.

C Paris.

10 WHAT IS THE NAME OF GARGAMEL'S NEW WAND?

A Wanda.

B Magico 2000.

C Alakazanimal.

9 SMURFETTE, VEXY AND HACKUS TAKE A RIDE ON WHICH ANIMALS?

A Some storks.

B Azrael.

C Some ducks.

11 WHY DID GARGAMEL CHOOSE PARIS FOR HIS HEADQUARTERS?

A He has always loved French food and wants to visit art galleries.

B He intends to use the Eiffel Tower as a giant transmitter.

C Azrael has fond memories of a holiday he once spent there as a kitten.

12 SMURFETTE IS CONFUSED. WHY?

A She is unsure whether she is a proper Smurf or Gargamel's daughter.

B She doesn't understand why she is the only Smurf who is a girl.

C She likes French fashion and is unsure whether she wants to go home.

HOW DID YOU DO?

ANSWERS ON PAGE 77

CHECK OUT THE OTHER TWO CHALLENGES LATER IN THE ANNUAL!

JOIN THE DOTS

WHO ON EARTH IS THIS?
JOIN THE DOTS TO FIND OUT!

26 © Peyo

SMURFETTE'S FRENCH DRESSING

THE ONE GOOD THING ABOUT SMURFETTE BEING SMURFNAPPED IS THAT SHE FINDS HERSELF IN PARIS, ONE OF THE MOST BEAUTIFUL CITIES IN THE WORLD AND A CENTRE FOR WORLD FASHION. SMURFETTE IS LUCKY ENOUGH TO SEE A FEW MODELS WHILE SHE IS THERE. BUT WHAT SORT OF DRESS DO YOU THINK WOULD SUIT SMURFETTE THE BEST? COMPLETE THE PICTURE BELOW AND COLOUR IT IN TO GIVE SMURFETTE THE DRESS OF HER DREAMS!

GARGAMEL'S
Magical Mystery

PESKY OLD GARGAMEL! HE HAS USED HIS MAGIC TO MIX UP THE NAMES OF SOME OF OUR HEROES. CAN YOU UNSCRAMBLE EACH NAME AND WRITE THEM IN THE WHITE BOX?

IVY TAW

_ _ _ _ _ _ _

BIN RAY

_ _ _ _ _ _ _

CHORGUY

_ _ _ _ _ _ _ _ _ _

WEARING SCOWL

_ _ _ _ _ _ _ _ _ _ _ _

FARMS RUN TAR OR

_ _ _ _ _ _ _ _ _ _ _ _

ANSWERS ON PAGE 77

IN THE SHADOWS

WHICH OF THESE SILHOUETTES IS MINE?

The Smurfs go to Paris

FINDING HERSELF IN GARGAMEL'S SUITE IN PARIS, SMURFETTE WAS UNDENIABLY SCARED. BUT SHE WAS DETERMINED TO PUT ON A BRAVE FACE TOO.

"You're wasting your time, Gargamel!" she said defiantly. "Papa and the others are going to come for me!"

"I don't think so Smurfette," Gargamel said, polishing his wand thoughtfully. "I was the one who made you. You do remember, don't you?"

Smurfette grew upset. This is just what she had been thinking. Was she a real Smurf?

The wizard replied: "Smurfette, if you want to go "home", all I need you to do is one little, tiny, itsy-bitsy thing. Just provide the secret formula that Papa used to turn you into a Smurf. It would help us both.

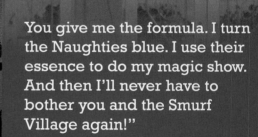

You give me the formula. I turn the Naughties blue. I use their essence to do my magic show. And then I'll never have to bother you and the Smurf Village again!"

"I don't believe you," Smurfette said. "I don't trust you. I'm not telling you anything."

Gargamel replied. "Very well then…Naughties attack!"

But the Naughties were so stupid they started fighting each other! Then the lamp. Then the cat.

Gargamel lowered his head. "Deeply, deeply disappointing experiments!" he said.

PART 2

Meanwhile, in the Smurf Village, Papa had called an emergency conference in his grotto. "Alright Smurfs. Listen up!" he said. "I saved some grotto water from the last blue moon for just such an occasion. I was able to smurf into smurfportation crystals."

"So we don't need a portal?" Brainy said.

"Smurf-zactly. These will take us directly to Master Winslow's apartment mushroom. If anyone can help us it's he and Miss Grace. I only had water enough for nine crystals. That's me and three others round trip, plus Smurfette on the way home. I'll need courage, strength and intelligence. So Gutsy, Hefty and Brainy – you'll smurf with me."

However, just as Papa prepared to hand over the crystals for travel, Clumsy accidentally knocked them. The three crystals flew into the open mouths of Vanity, Lazy and Grouchy! With a pop, pop, pop all three disappeared. Only Vanity's mirror was left.

Papa picked up the remaining crystals from the ground. He put them all in his satchel. Except one which he popped into his mouth.

"Smurf me luck!" he said. He was gone.

At the Winslow home, it was baby Blue Winslow's second birthday and the party had been a huge success.

Just then the front door swung open and a scruffy older man entered.

"Am I late? Did I miss the presents?" said the man. "All week I've been trying to figure out what to get Blue. Toys, games, electronics, sporting goods. Then suddenly I realised – I know, I'll get him everything!" he pulled in a red wagon laden down with far, far too many presents.

"Grandpa Vicster!" shouted Blue eagerly. But Patrick's heart sank. The new arrival was Victor, his stepfather. The couple made Victor welcome, but later they left him in the living room playing with Blue. They needed to talk alone in the bedroom.

"What is he doing here?" Patrick asked Grace.

"It's Blue's birthday. I invited him!" his wife replied. "Honey, Blue needs to learn that "family" means more than just you and me.

It's good for him to play with his grandfather."

"Step-grandfather," Patrick reminded her. "Grace, he ruins everything. It's like when he first moved into my house and sent my parrot away."

Grace was confused. "Your parrot?"

"My father's parrot. When my dad left…it was the only thing which he left behind. I loved that bird. It used to ride around on my handlebars. Sleep on my heardboard. But when Vic came along he had to get rid of him because he was allergic."

Just then, they were disturbed by a bizarre WOOMF, WOOMF, WOOMF noise. Grace looked out of the window. "Helicopter?" Grace said. But it wasn't.

In the living room, Vic and Blue were disturbed by the noise too. Suddenly a comet flew in through the window and crashed into the pile of presents. It was actually the Smurf, Grouchy.

Outside Grace and Patrick were frantic. "Vic! Do you have Blue?" Some sort of pressure was preventing them from opening the door.

THE SMURFS WERE ARRIVING. Within seconds, two more comets had crashed in, one containing Clumsy, the other Vanity. A final comet containing Papa Smurf arrived seconds later. Patrick recognised the familiar Smurfs' voices from outside. Pressure returned to normal and Patrick and Grace suddenly fell through the door into the room.

But they were horrified to see that Uncle Vic, who had never seen Smurfs before was attacking them with a toy light sabre. "Victor! Stop! They're friends!" said Patrick.

"Friends?!?" snorted Vic. "They're little blue aliens trying to steal our faces!"

"No, they're Smurfs!" said Grace, picking up Grouchy. "And they're the sweetest things you'll ever meet"

Blue started pointing and calling out. "Smoofs! Smoofs! Smoofs!". "That's right, Blue. These are the Smurfs we've told you about, " Patrick said.

"If Blue likes the Smurfs then Vicster likes the Smurfs!" laughed Vic.

"So what are you guys doing here?" asked Patrick. Papa Smurf told them about Smurfette and how she had been kidnapped by Gargamel. The Winslows already knew the wizard was in France as they had heard of Gargamel's world famous magic show.

The Smurf group had set off by plane to the French capital of Paris. The rescue had begun.

Meanwhile, in his dressing room in the Paris Opera House, Gargamel was attempting to hypnotise Smurfette to make her give him the formula. It wasn't working and Gargamel was getting desperate. He needed more essence and fast for tonight's performance. He picked up a pair of scissors and headed for Smurfette.

Then, to Smurfette's horror, he cut a large swathe of her hair.

"So either you can give your real Papa – that is, me - the formula," Gargamel continued, "or you can spend the rest of your miserable existence being harvested in my new super-powered Smurfalator!" The mad wizard laughed evilly. "As soon as she gives up the secret, I'm going to toss her into the machine for a long life of pain, torture and suffering."

He turned his attention to the Naughties. "While I am gone, Vexy, keep at her. Her brain has been washed. You must unwash it."

Vexy agreed. Gargamel went on: "And if you see any blue Smurfs around, take no chances!" Gargamel slid open a panel in the wall and began to prepare more essence. Smurfette meanwhile gazed at her own half cut hair in the reflection on the vase. She could only sob. She had never felt so alone.

© Peyo

However, not far away, the others were working towards her rescue. Patrick had sneaked into the theatre with the Smurfs inside his jacket.

"Okay Papa," Patrick said. "Sneak out of the back of my jacket while I'm talking to this man and find the dressing room.

The Smurfs sneaked past the guard and were making their way across the rigging backstage.

"This whole thing's going to be a Smurf-tastrophe!" Grouchy said.

Meanwhile, Gargamel was performing on stage when Azrael suddenly walked on. The audience began to laugh much to the magician's displeasure.

"Stop that! Why do you chortle?" Gargamel shouted.

"The cat is so small"!" a man in the front row shouted.

"In magic, cats are usually very big, no? Lions, tigers…"

"Silence knaves!" the mad sorcerer interrupted. "If it is a big cat you crave so be it…Alakazanimal!" he said.

The audience went wild with applause. Azrael was suddenly twice the size of a tiger!

At that moment, the Naughties were discussing what to do with Smurfette and how to get her to talk.

"Alright, here's my plan," Vexy said. "We trick her into being naughty. Use all he goodness against her. Once that happens, she'll feel like one of us and then…"

But Smurfette was planning her own escape. She had managed to push the glass bottle in which she was trapped, towards the edge of the table. It now toppled over, shattering on the ground. Free at last, Smurfette escaped into a nearby air vent.

"Oh no! Get her!" Vexy said.

On stage Gargamel was desperate to get a volunteer from the audience.

"Oh come now!" he appealed. "One little volunteer to stick their head in little kitty's mouth! There's a very good chance you'll survive."

Patrick approached the stage ...but who should walk onto the stage just before him but Victor! He quickly handed Blue to Patrick and then approached Gargamel on stage. "Yo magic man!" he said boldly to Gargamel. "Hand over the Smurf-it!"

Gargamel raised his wand to fire. "Who are you? How dare you?" he said.

"Duck!" shouted Patrick to Victor. "Duck?" said Gargamel. A blue beam fired out of his wand and the next second Vic was transformed...into a duck!

"Alright – I did not see that one coming!" said Vic as the audience broke into applause.

Patrick shouted in shock. But this only drew Gargamel's attention towards him. "You! I know you!" Gargamel said and zapped Patrick with his wand. Patrick just had time to put Blue down before he started floating high above the crowd. "It appears we have a volunteer at last ladies and gentlemen!" Gargamel said. "Open wide Azrael!" As Patrick floated towards the giant cat, the crowd went wild. Azrael opened his mouth and roared.

But Victor, though a duck, was enraged. "Put him down!" he yelled, flying madly at the crazed wizard and knocking him to the floor. Abruptly, the energy beam coming from the wand ended too and Patrick fell to Earth with a bump. Right in front of a hungry-looking giant Azrael! Fortunately a random wand blast from the struggling Gargamel transformed Azrael back to his normal size. Patrick quickly seized Blue and fled while Victor dodged Gargamel's wand blasts and escaped too.

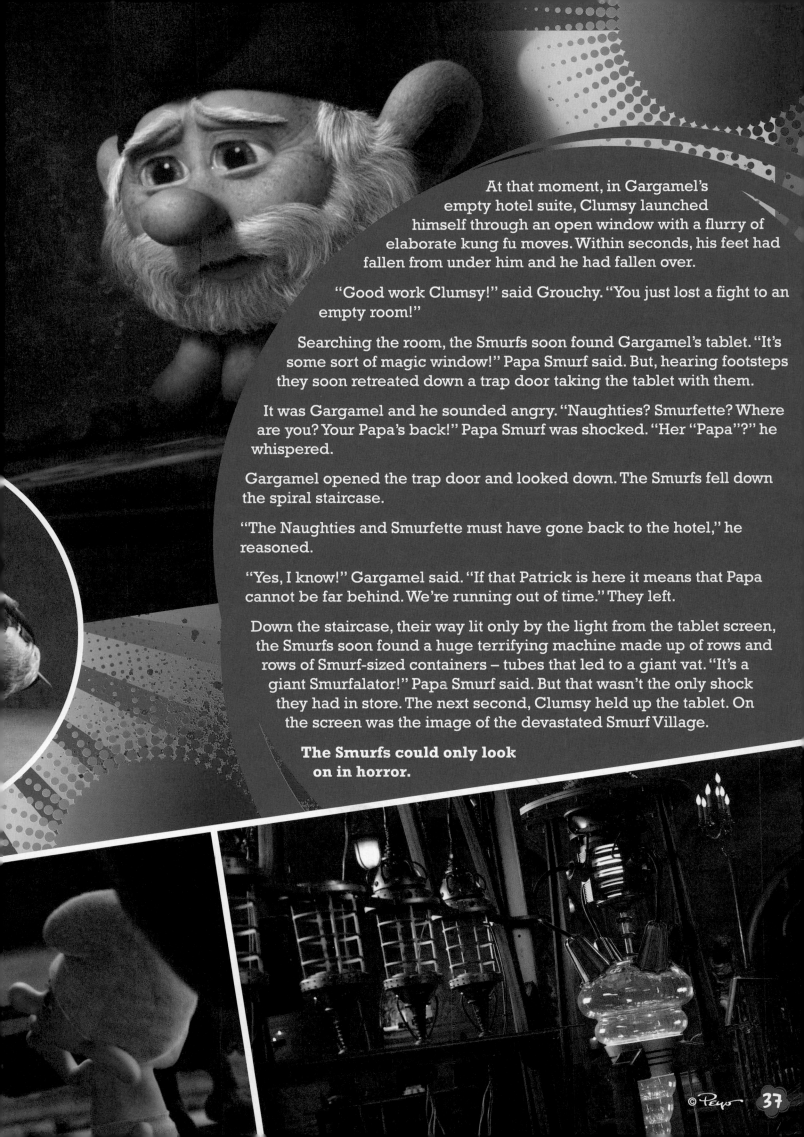

At that moment, in Gargamel's empty hotel suite, Clumsy launched himself through an open window with a flurry of elaborate kung fu moves. Within seconds, his feet had fallen from under him and he had fallen over.

"Good work Clumsy!" said Grouchy. "You just lost a fight to an empty room!"

Searching the room, the Smurfs soon found Gargamel's tablet. "It's some sort of magic window!" Papa Smurf said. But, hearing footsteps they soon retreated down a trap door taking the tablet with them.

It was Gargamel and he sounded angry. "Naughties? Smurfette? Where are you? Your Papa's back!" Papa Smurf was shocked. "Her "Papa"?" he whispered.

Gargamel opened the trap door and looked down. The Smurfs fell down the spiral staircase.

"The Naughties and Smurfette must have gone back to the hotel," he reasoned.

"Yes, I know!" Gargamel said. "If that Patrick is here it means that Papa cannot be far behind. We're running out of time." They left.

Down the staircase, their way lit only by the light from the tablet screen, the Smurfs soon found a huge terrifying machine made up of rows and rows of Smurf-sized containers – tubes that led to a giant vat. "It's a giant Smurfalator!" Papa Smurf said. But that wasn't the only shock they had in store. The next second, Clumsy held up the tablet. On the screen was the image of the devastated Smurf Village.

The Smurfs could only look on in horror.

VANITY'S MYSTERY MIRROR

SILLY OLD VANITY LIKES NOTHING BETTER THAN GAZING AT HIS OWN REFLECTION. TROUBLE IS, GARGAMEL HAS CAST A SPELL ON HIS MIRROR. ONLY ONE OF THE MIRROR IMAGES BELOW CONTAINS VANITY'S TRUE REFLECTION. CAN YOU SPOT WHICH ONE?

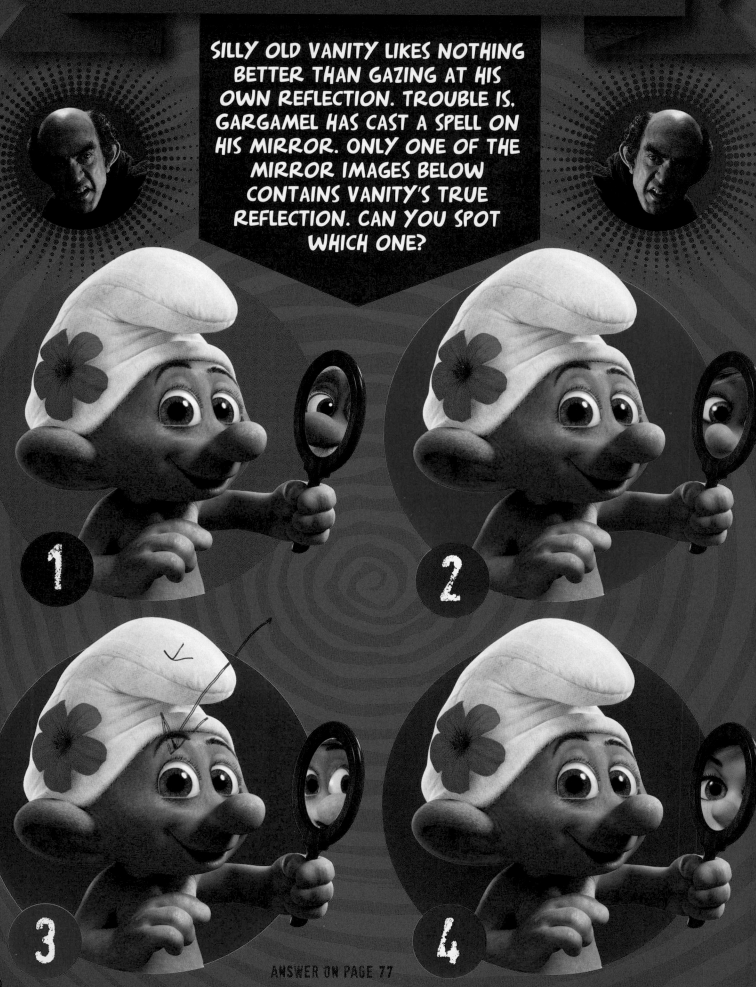

ANSWER ON PAGE 77

LOOK WHO'S TALKING?

SMURFS (AND OTHER CHARACTERS) SAY THE FUNNIEST THINGS! CAN YOU MATCH THESE QUOTES WITH THE CHARACTERS?

"I GET SO PUFFY WHEN I TRAVEL!"
....

"EVERY YEAR I HAVE THESE HORRIBLE DREAMS AND THEY REMIND ME HOW DIFFERENT I AM."
....

"DEEPLY, DEEPLY DISAPPOINTING EXPERIMENTS."
....

"IT'S NOT IN A DUCK'S NATURE TO GET UPSET. WE LET THINGS...ROLL OFF OUR BACKS."
....

"NO, WE'RE IN THE ABYSS! I KNEW IT WOULD END LIKE THIS!"
....

"MEEEOWW!"
....

"IT DOESN'T MATTER WHERE YOU CAME FROM. WHAT MATTERS IS WHO YOU CHOOSE TO BE."
....

"IT WAS A DAY WE WILL NEVER FORGET. THE DAY OUR SMURFETTE WAS REBORN."
....

"IS A SMURF'S BUTT BLUE?"
....

ANSWERS ON PAGE 77

Exclusive Poster

Brainy's
CHALLENGE PART 2

1 WHICH OF THESE SMURFS DOES NOT GO TO PARIS?

- **A** Hefty.
- **B** Vanity.
- **C** Papa Smurf.

2 WHAT IS THE NAME OF PATRICK & GRACE'S BABY?

- **A** Patrick Junior.
- **B** Blue.
- **C** Victor.

3 SMURFETTE HAS A BAD DREAM AT THE START OF THE STORY. WHAT CAUSES IT?

- **A** He needs Smurf essence to fuel his magic tricks and work towards taking over the world.
- **B** He secretly wants to become a Smurf himself.
- **C** He doesn't. He is distracting Smurfette while he plots greater acts of evil.

GOOD LUCK

4 IN WHAT SORT OF SHOP DOES HACKUS GET INTO TROUBLE?

- **A** A toy shop.
- **B** A department store.
- **C** A sweet shop.

5 WHICH OF THESE SMURFS IS NOT ALMOST SWALLOWED BY PATRICK AND GRACE'S BABY?

- **A** Clumsy.
- **B** Grouchy.
- **C** Vanity.

© Peyo

FEELING CLEVER? THEN TEST OUT YOUR SMURFING KNOWLEDGE WITH THIS QUIZ FROM THE CLEVEREST SMURF IN THE VILLAGE, BRAINY.

CIRCLE THE CORRECT ANSWER FROM THE CHOICES AVAILABLE. THEN TOT UP YOUR SCORE. GOOD LUCK!

6 WHY DON'T ANY OF THE SMURFS WANT TO GO FOR A WALK WITH SMURFETTE AT THE START OF THE STORY?

A They don't like her - she is Gargamel's daughter.

B They are busy planning her surprise party.

C They are busy preparing to go to Paris.

7 GRACE REVEALS SHE GREW UP WHERE?

A Canada.

B France.

C The UK.

8 WHO WAS ZEUS?

A Patrick's childhood companion parrot.

B One of the Naughties.

C Patrick's actual father.

9 WHY DOES SMURFETTE APOLOGISE TO PAPA SMURF TOWARDS THE END?

A For getting kidnapped.

B For giving Gargamel the formula.

C For riding on a stork.

10 WHO CATCHES THE FALLING SMURFS?

A Grace.

B Hefty.

C Victor.

11 VEXY & HACKUS ARE:

A Friends.

B Mother and son.

C Sister and brother.

12 WHICH FAIRGROUND RIDE DO GARGAMEL AND SMURFETTE DISRUPT?

A A Ferris wheel.

B The dodgems.

C The helter skelter.

HOW DID YOU DO?

ANSWERS ON PAGE 77

HAVE YOU COMPLETED THE CHALLENGE ON PAGE 26?

SPELLMAKER

TRULY GARGAMEL IS A REVOLTING CHARACTER! BUT HOW MANY SHORTER WORDS CAN YOU MAKE OUT OF HIS NAME BELOW? WRITE DOWN YOUR ANSWERS IN THE BOX – WE HAVE ALREADY DONE TWO TO GET YOU STARTED...

GARGAMEL LE GREAT

Tear
Rage

© Peyo

Colour it in!

WHAT A SMURFTASTIC SCENE! COLOUR IN THE PICTURE BELOW OF VANITY'S FRIENDS USING EITHER THE CORRECT COLOURS (SUCH AS BLUE FOR SMURFS!) OR USE ANY COLOURS YOU LIKE. HAPPY COLOURING!

SMURF TASTIC!

45

Hide &

© Peyo

Seek

ANSWER ON PAGE 77

DRAW A NEW Naughtie!

GARGAMEL IS DISAPPOINTED WITH HOW THE NAUGHTIES HACKUS AND VEXY HAVE TURNED OUT. HE WANTS YOU TO DRAW HIM A NEW ONE (BOY OR GIRL) IN THE SPACE BELOW. CAN YOU HELP HIM? AND CAN YOU THINK OF A NAME FOR YOUR NEW NAUGHTIE?

NAME: Lucy

ABC
BRAINY'S A+ MATHS PUZZLER

Brainy is the cleverest Smurf. Can you complete his mathematical challenge?

The number of Naughties

x multiplied by x

The number of Smurfs who go to Paris to rescue Smurfette

+ plus +

The age of Blue on his birthday

- take away -

The number of storks flown on

= equals... =

WHAT ANSWER DO YOU GET?

?

Smurfe
in Trouble

SMURFETTE WAS ON THE RUN. RUNNING DOWN A NARROW STREET.

Hot on her tail, the Naughties chanced upon an old fashioned sweet shop. Vexy pointed it out to Hackus. "Go get yourself in trouble," she said. "Even you can manage that."

HACKUS GREW EXCITED: "TROUBLE! TROUBLE! HACKUS LOVE TROUBLE!"

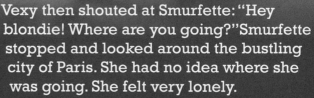

Vexy then shouted at Smurfette: "Hey blondie! Where are you going?" Smurfette stopped and looked around the bustling city of Paris. She had no idea where she was going. She felt very lonely.

"Aren't you tired of being alone?" Vexy asked. "I don't know how you did it, living in that village. I could never live somewhere I didn't belong." Smurfette was listening. Did Vexy understand her?

"I didn't kidnap you, Smurfette. I brought you home".

Suddenly, they heard screams. Hackus was going wild in the sweetshop. He stuck his head in the candy floss machine, pulling it out to reveal a lovely candy floss hairstyle. He swung round on a liquorice whip. He generally went berserk.

Smurfette was alarmed. "Oh my God! He's going to be killed! We have to help! But…" she paused.

"I thought you were supposed to be good?" said Vexy.

In the sweet shop, the employees had Hackus cornered. Then Smurfette charged in and with Vexy's help flicked a spatula at one of the girls and pushed Hackus onto a cart. The three made their escape. "Nice move! Stealing a cart!" said Vexy as they trundled away. "I didn't steal it," said Smurfette. "It's not yours is it? See you're just like us."

The cart containing Smurfette and the Naughties suddenly crashed into a puddle. Hackus immediately took a slurp. "Yum, pudding!" he said.

Nearby, Smurfette spotted some fashion models dressed as storks. Each one was holding a bundled baby. Nearby were some actual storks too. "Quick! Get on the storks!" said Smurfette, eagerly running over. Hackus, confused as ever, leapt on an actual model instead!

"Can you believe we're related to him?" joked Vexy as the model screamed flapping at Hackus frantically.

"No Hackus! A real stork!" Smurfette shouted. Soon all three were on storks although Hackus was facing the wrong way.

"I can see forever!" shouted Vexy. She was genuinely excited. The Naughties had never done anything like this before.

C'est Si Bon

"Did you do this with your sisters at the Smurf Village?" Vexy asked.

"I did! But I never had a sister." said Smurfette. "Well, you do now!"

"Hackus happy! Hackus happy!" shouted Hackus as they swooped towards the Mini Statue of Liberty.

"Wow! They've got one of these everywhere!" Smurfette said.

Meanwhile, the other Smurfs updated each other back at the Winslows' hotel room.

"How did it go?" Grace asked.

"It was a complete Smurf-wreck," said Grouchy.

"No, it wasn't," said Clumsy. "We didn't find Smurfette but at least we know Gargamel's plan."

He explained that Gargamel was trying to get the secret formula out of Smurfette.

"But Smurfette would never tell him," said Grace. "Right Papa?" Papa was worried but tried to hide it. "Uh…of course not. There's nothing to worry about there."

Patrick also explained how Victor had been turned into a duck.

"Can you turn him back?" Grace asked Papa Smurf anxiously.

"It's a transformation spell, "said Papa. "It can only last so long."

Patrick suddenly sneezed. "And now I'm catching a cold."

"Of course you are!" moaned Grouchy. "Everything that can go wrong, will. It's Smurfy's Law!"

"Would you stop being so negative?" Clumsy said.

"I'm not negative, I'm…" but suddenly Grouchy realised he was.

"Listen to me, Grouchy-guy," said Victor. "Nobody ever accomplished anything positive by being negative. Okay?"

"Grace explained she had and a plan to get to Gargamel's room.

Later, in the living room, Patrick attempted to rally the Smurfs. "We're going to get Smurfette this time. One hundred percent guaranteed!" said Grouchy.

"What did you just say, Grouchy?" said Papa Smurf.

© Peyo

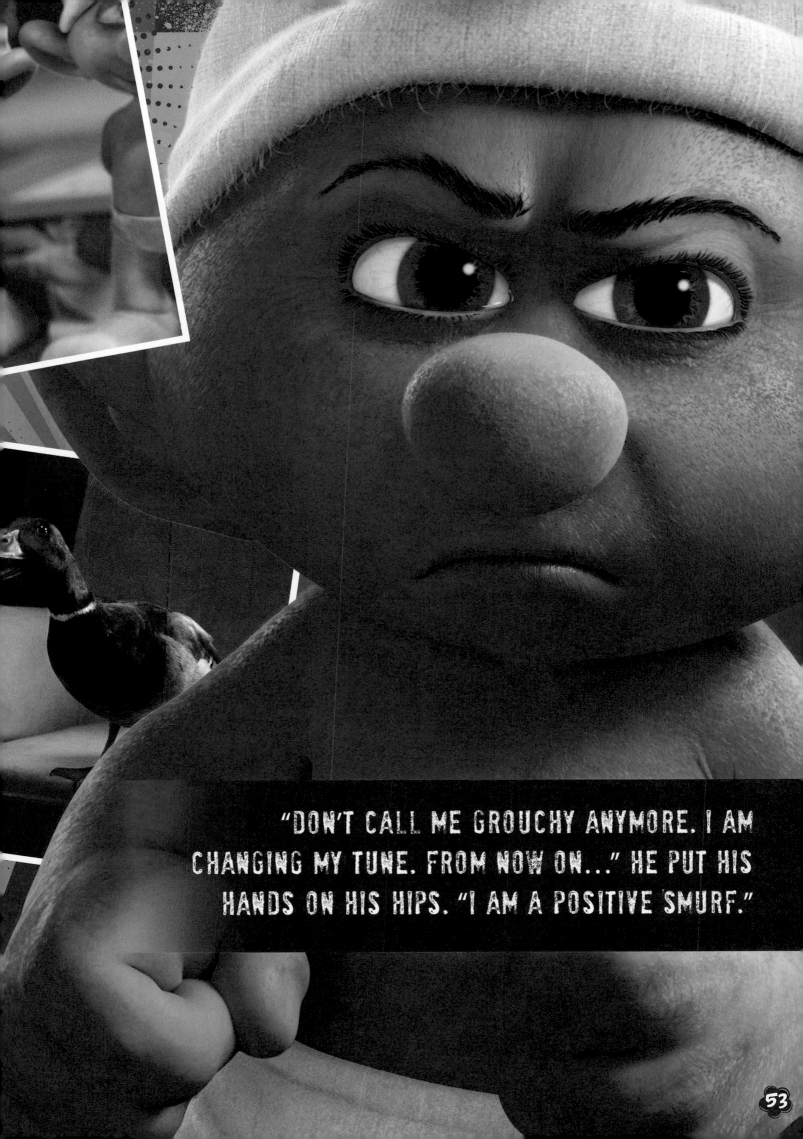

"DON'T CALL ME GROUCHY ANYMORE. I AM CHANGING MY TUNE. FROM NOW ON..." HE PUT HIS HANDS ON HIS HIPS. "I AM A POSITIVE SMURF."

Meanwhile, Patrick did an impressive impression of Gargamel on the phone: "Listen well, you slack-jawed knave," he said, copying the wizard's rude manner as he called room service. "I want ale, curds and blistered meats sent to my room in ten minutes – or I will turn you into a legless tree sloth!" The Smurfs were impressed.

But not everyone was happy. Victor was bored. He had been ordered to stay back at their hotel by Patrick while the others attempted to rescue Smurfette. But then…what was that? He'd spotted Patrick's key card on the floor! Patrick must have dropped it by accident from his uniform! Vic had to return it to him.

Patrick, meanwhile, was pushing a trolley disguised as a waiter delivering room service to Gargamel's room. The Smurfs accompanied him. "Okay guys, "briefed Patrick. "When we do get to the room, if there's any problem…" "There's no such thing as problems, my friend," Grouchy said. "Only Smurfitunities."

"You're freaking me out, Grouchy," Vanity said.

"I'm Positive Smurf!" said Grouchy angrily.

Just then, as Patrick stuck his head out of the lift door who should he see but Victor the duck hiding behind a plant!

"What are you doing here?" asked Patrick, stepping out of the lift briefly and leaving the others behind.

"Saving your tail feather!" Vic said. "It's the security card for the elevator." Patrick looked at the card. "I already have the security card. That's our room key."

"Oh," said Vic, crestfallen. "Well, now when you come back, you'll be able to get in – no problem."

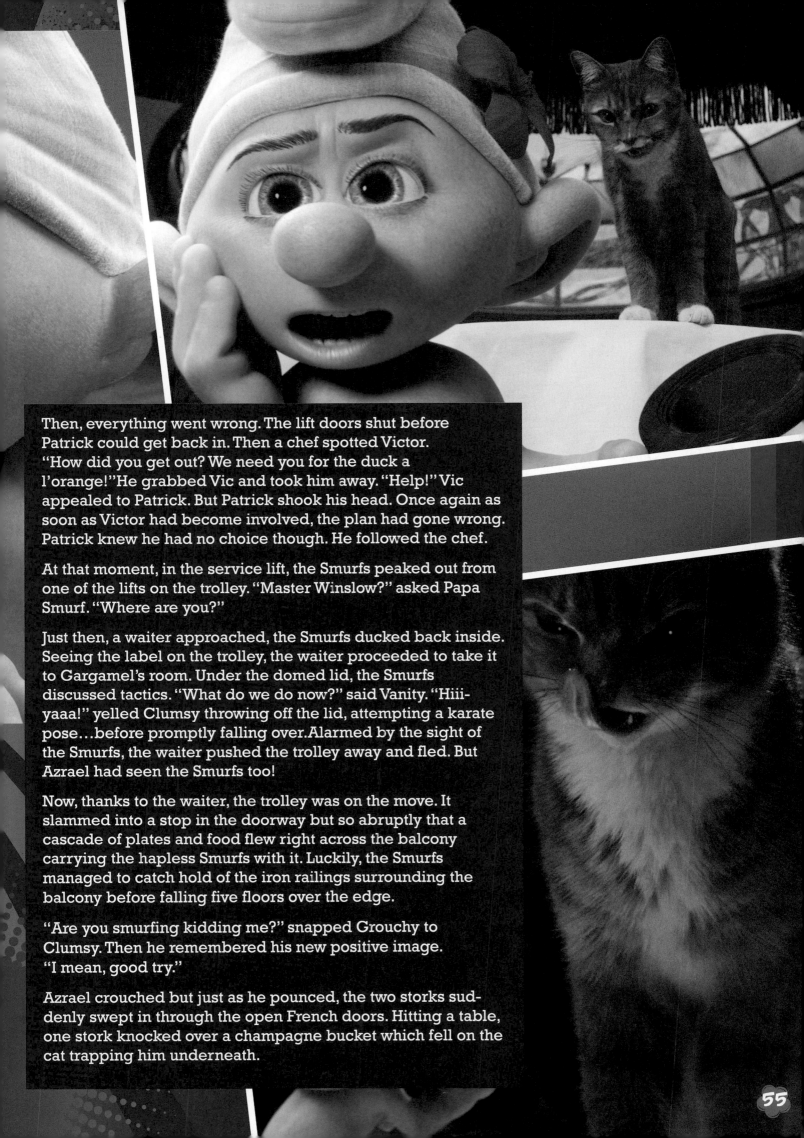

Then, everything went wrong. The lift doors shut before Patrick could get back in. Then a chef spotted Victor. "How did you get out? We need you for the duck a l'orange!" He grabbed Vic and took him away. "Help!" Vic appealed to Patrick. But Patrick shook his head. Once again as soon as Victor had become involved, the plan had gone wrong. Patrick knew he had no choice though. He followed the chef.

At that moment, in the service lift, the Smurfs peaked out from one of the lifts on the trolley. "Master Winslow?" asked Papa Smurf. "Where are you?"

Just then, a waiter approached, the Smurfs ducked back inside. Seeing the label on the trolley, the waiter proceeded to take it to Gargamel's room. Under the domed lid, the Smurfs discussed tactics. "What do we do now?" said Vanity. "Hiii-yaaa!" yelled Clumsy throwing off the lid, attempting a karate pose…before promptly falling over. Alarmed by the sight of the Smurfs, the waiter pushed the trolley away and fled. But Azrael had seen the Smurfs too!

Now, thanks to the waiter, the trolley was on the move. It slammed into a stop in the doorway but so abruptly that a cascade of plates and food flew right across the balcony carrying the hapless Smurfs with it. Luckily, the Smurfs managed to catch hold of the iron railings surrounding the balcony before falling five floors over the edge.

"Are you smurfing kidding me?" snapped Grouchy to Clumsy. Then he remembered his new positive image. "I mean, good try."

Azrael crouched but just as he pounced, the two storks suddenly swept in through the open French doors. Hitting a table, one stork knocked over a champagne bucket which fell on the cat trapping him underneath.

"That will do, stork," said Smurfette. The Naughties shooed the storks away and shut and locked the doors shut behind them. All were very excited from the adventure they just had. They hadn't even noticed the other Smurfs on the balcony outside.

"That was awesome! High fours!" said Vexy as they smacked their hands together. Smurfette suddenly felt very close to Vexy and began to hug her. But Vexy was caught unawares.

"What are you doing?!?"

"I'm just hugging you," Smurfette said, letting go. "Haven't you ever been hugged before?" Hackus joined in and soon all three were hugging. Looking in from the balcony, the other Smurfs were confused.

"There she is!" said Clumsy, "But she's hugging the pale Smurfs!"

"What is she doing?" said Grouchy.

"See? Now that's the real you," said Vexy pointing to Smurfette's tatty and dirty image reflected in the glass door. She fitted in with the Naughties perfectly.

Outside, the other Smurfs attempted to get her attention. But the reflection on the door was too strong and she could neither see nor hear them. "Wow! She's really let herself go." Said Vanity.

"She's confused," said Papa. "Help me get this door open."

"It's called Smurf-holme Syndrome," said Grouchy. "You become sympathetic to your captors."

"We have to get her before she turns!" said Papa.

© Peyo

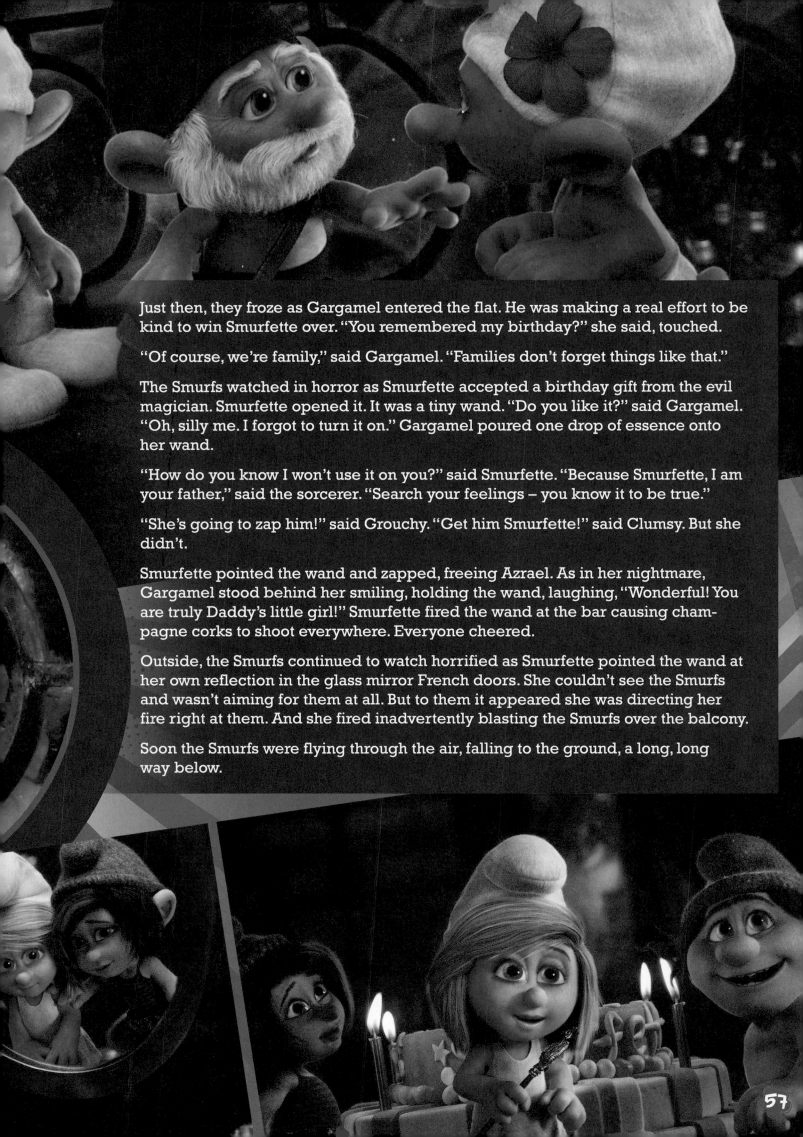

Just then, they froze as Gargamel entered the flat. He was making a real effort to be kind to win Smurfette over. "You remembered my birthday?" she said, touched.

"Of course, we're family," said Gargamel. "Families don't forget things like that."

The Smurfs watched in horror as Smurfette accepted a birthday gift from the evil magician. Smurfette opened it. It was a tiny wand. "Do you like it?" said Gargamel. "Oh, silly me. I forgot to turn it on." Gargamel poured one drop of essence onto her wand.

"How do you know I won't use it on you?" said Smurfette. "Because Smurfette, I am your father," said the sorcerer. "Search your feelings – you know it to be true."

"She's going to zap him!" said Grouchy. "Get him Smurfette!" said Clumsy. But she didn't.

Smurfette pointed the wand and zapped, freeing Azrael. As in her nightmare, Gargamel stood behind her smiling, holding the wand, laughing, "Wonderful! You are truly Daddy's little girl!" Smurfette fired the wand at the bar causing champagne corks to shoot everywhere. Everyone cheered.

Outside, the Smurfs continued to watch horrified as Smurfette pointed the wand at her own reflection in the glass mirror French doors. She couldn't see the Smurfs and wasn't aiming for them at all. But to them it appeared she was directing her fire right at them. And she fired inadvertently blasting the Smurfs over the balcony.

Soon the Smurfs were flying through the air, falling to the ground, a long, long way below.

Escape FROM Paris!

CAN YOU HELP SMURFETTE ESCAPE FROM GARGAMEL'S LAIR AND RETURN TO SAFETY?

SAFETY!

22

YOU GET LOST ON THE PARIS UNDERGROUND! GO BACK TO 3!

HOW MANY PEOPLE ARE PLAYING? MOVE BACK BY THAT NUMBER!

13

AZRAEL SPOTS YOU! RUN BACK TO THE START!
<<<<

11

A SPELL BY GARGAMEL TURNS YOU INTO A DUCK! GO BACK 4 SPACES WHILE YOU TURN BACK.

9

START HERE

1

VEXY IS HERE! GO BACK TO THE START
<<<<

TO PLAY THIS GAME YOU WILL NEED A DICE, SOME COUNTERS AND AT LEAST ONE OTHER PERSON.
THE YOUNGEST PLAYER STARTS THE GAME! — ROLL A DICE, THEN MOVE YOUR COUNTER TO THE APPROPRIATE SQUARE
AND FOLLOW ANY INSTRUCTIONS GIVEN. THE WINNER IS THE FIRST ONE TO GET SMURFETTE TO FINAL SQUARE SAFETY.
IF YOU ROLL TOO HIGH A NUMBER TO GET TO THE FINAL SQUARE, YOU MUST STAY PUT AND ROLL AGAIN NEXT TURN!

20

GARGAMEL HYPNOTISES
YOU. MISS A TURN!

18

IS IT THE
WEEKEND? IF SO,
GO AHEAD 3
SPACES.
OTHERWISE,
STAY PUT.

16

ROLL
AGAIN

8

ARE YOU
WEARING ANY
CLOTHES WITH
BLUE ON THEM?
IF SO, ADVANCE
TO 20!

6

4

YOU
SNEAK
PAST
HACKUS.
ROLL
AGAIN

CLIMB THE EIFFEL
TOWER TO 8

59

CLOSE-UPS!

CAN YOU IDENTIFY THESE 7 DIFFERENT SMURFS FROM THE ENLARGED CLOSE UP PICTURES OF THEM?

1 ANSWER:

Vexy

2 ANSWER: Brainy

~~Brainy~~

3 ANSWER:

Healfy

ANSWERS ON PAGE 77

60

ANSWER:
Smet

4

ANSWER:
Grouchy

5

6

ANSWER:
hackus

ANSWER:
papa

7

Victor's

© Peyo

QUACKERS JOKES

WHERE DO BABY
MONKEYS SLEEP?
IN AN APRICOT!

WHERE DO HORSES GO
WHEN THEY ARE UNWELL?
TO HORSE-PITAL!

WHY DO BIRDS FLY
SOUTH IN THE WINTER?
BECAUSE IT'S TOO
FAR TO WALK!

WHY DID THE DINOSAUR
CROSS THE ROAD?
BECAUSE THEY DIDN'T HAVE
CHICKENS BACK THEN!

WHAT'S A COW'S FAVOURITE PROGRAMME?
THE SIX O'CLOCK MOOS!

WHAT DID THE DALMATIAN SAY TO THE POODLE?
NOTHING, DOGS CAN'T TALK!

HELP SMURFETTE REMEMBER...

HELP! SMURFETTE HAS BEEN IN CAPTIVITY FOR SO LONG SHE IS STARTING TO FORGET THE OTHER SMURFS! USE THE CLUES BELOW TO HELP JOG HER MEMORY OF THEM...

A BIT OF A KNOW-IT-ALL.

HE HAS A HEART OF GOLD UNDERNEATH ALL THE GRUMPINESS.

HE'S NEVER WITHOUT HIS MIRROR

THE STRONGEST SMURF?

HE'S ALWAYS THERE WITH GOOD ADVICE.

HIS KUNG FU MOVES REALLY ARE A JOKE

ANSWERS ON PAGE 77

HEFTY'S QUIZ

THINK YOU KNOW YOUR SMURFS? TEST YOUR SMUFING KNOWLEDGE BY ANSWERING TRUE OR FALSE TO EACH OF THESE STATEMENTS FROM HEFTY...

TRUE

OR FALSE

1 SMURFETTE IS THE ONLY FEMALE SMURF?

....

2 GARGAMEL SECRETLY HAS A HEART OF GOLD?

....

3 BLUE IS THE YOUNGEST SMURF OF ALL?

....

4 PAPA SMURF IS OVER 500 YEARS OLD?

....

5 VANITY WAS ACTUALLY CREATED BY GARGAMEL?

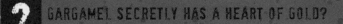

....

6 MOST OF THIS STORY TAKES PLACE IN EUROPE?

....

7 BRAINY IS THE ONLY SMURF WITH A BEARD?

....

8 AZRAEL IS ONE OF THE NAUGHTIES?

....

9 GARGAMEL USED TO BE A SMURF?

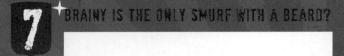

....

10 HEFTY DEVISED THIS QUIZ?

....

CLUMSY'S MIX UP

SILLY CLUMSY HAS MESSED UP AGAIN! HE WAS GIVEN A LIST OF CHARACTERS TO LOOK AFTER BUT HAS MANAGED TO TOTALLY JUMBLE THEM UP! CAN YOU HELP HIM TO UNSCRAMBLE THESE NAMES BEFORE THE OTHER SMURFS GET BACK?

FAR UP MAPS

....

FEET STRUM

....

NITPICK SLOW WAR

....

OILED

....

ZEALAR

....

ANSWERS ON PAGE 77

The Smurfs to the Rescue

Thankfully, Patrick's rescue of Victor from the hotel kitchens turned out to be a straightforward matter. Despite this, Patrick was still annoyed with his stepfather. But as they emerged from the hotel onto the plaza, they heard screams from above. The Smurfs were falling to Earth!

Vic flew up to catch them but as he did so – poof! – he suddenly turned back into a human! The Smurfs bounced off his back and fell into a nearby laundry bin. Victor now had no clothes on so hid under the clothes himself. Vanity was deeply embarrassed to be in such a mess. But at least the Smurfs had been saved.

Back at Patrick's hotel room, Patrick was updating the Smurfs. He was also still clearly angry with Victor. "We almost found Smurfette but HE messed it up. We were so close and now

"We almost found Smurfette but HE messed it up. We were so close and now there's no telling what Gargamel has done to her! I want him gone!"

"I'm not your father," said Victor. The others looked round. He had emerged from the bedroom and was now fully dressed. "Your real father left and started a new family. And you're mad about that – and you should be – I'm sick and tired of you blaming me for it!"

"What about Zeus?" said Patrick.

"Zeus? The pigeon?"

"The parrot. My parrot. You took him away because you were allergic!" Victor explained. "I was not allergic to that bird!" he said. "You were!"

Now Patrick was confused as Victor explained. "Every day you would wheeze as a result of the bird feathers. But your mother and I knew it would break your heart to think that bird had to go away because of you. You already blamed yourself for your father. So I took the heat."

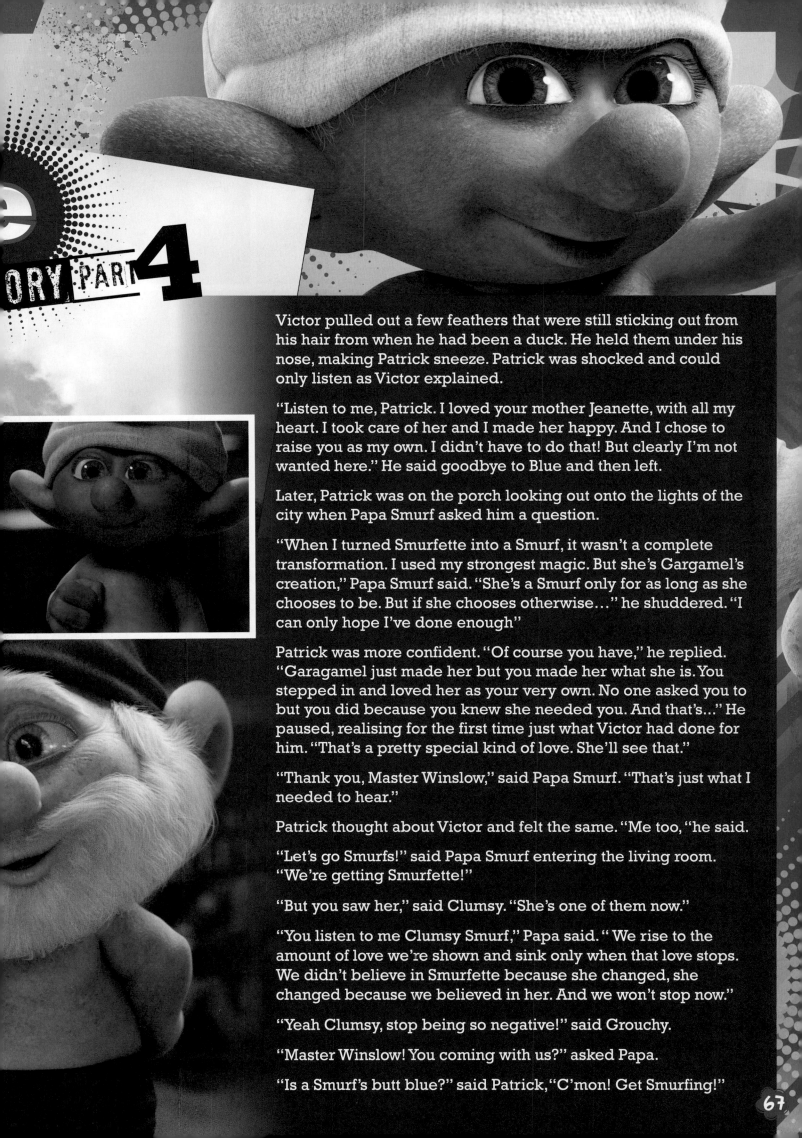

Victor pulled out a few feathers that were still sticking out from his hair from when he had been a duck. He held them under his nose, making Patrick sneeze. Patrick was shocked and could only listen as Victor explained.

"Listen to me, Patrick. I loved your mother Jeanette, with all my heart. I took care of her and I made her happy. And I chose to raise you as my own. I didn't have to do that! But clearly I'm not wanted here." He said goodbye to Blue and then left.

Later, Patrick was on the porch looking out onto the lights of the city when Papa Smurf asked him a question.

"When I turned Smurfette into a Smurf, it wasn't a complete transformation. I used my strongest magic. But she's Gargamel's creation," Papa Smurf said. "She's a Smurf only for as long as she chooses to be. But if she chooses otherwise…" he shuddered. "I can only hope I've done enough"

Patrick was more confident. "Of course you have," he replied. "Garagamel just made her but you made her what she is. You stepped in and loved her as your very own. No one asked you to but you did because you knew she needed you. And that's…" He paused, realising for the first time just what Victor had done for him. "That's a pretty special kind of love. She'll see that."

"Thank you, Master Winslow," said Papa Smurf. "That's just what I needed to hear."

Patrick thought about Victor and felt the same. "Me too, "he said.

"Let's go Smurfs!" said Papa Smurf entering the living room. "We're getting Smurfette!"

"But you saw her," said Clumsy. "She's one of them now."

"You listen to me Clumsy Smurf," Papa said. " We rise to the amount of love we're shown and sink only when that love stops. We didn't believe in Smurfette because she changed, she changed because we believed in her. And we won't stop now."

"Yeah Clumsy, stop being so negative!" said Grouchy.

"Master Winslow! You coming with us?" asked Papa.

"Is a Smurf's butt blue?" said Patrick, "C'mon! Get Smurfing!"

That night in Gargamel's underground lair, Gargamel led the Naughties into his laboratory where the giant evil Smurfalator was kept.

"Today is your sister's birthday," the mad wizard said. "We can't very well celebrate without a cake." With a flash of his wand, candles lit up a birthday cake which floated over and landed in front of Smurfette.

"It's your favourite, Smurfette, blue velvet," Gargamel said. "Now make a wish. Of course, all I need is the formula so that I can make it so."

Meanwhile, the other Smurfs had sneaked in through a sewer grate and were looking down from a fenced in ledge in the lab, high above.

Papa told Vanity to come with him, while Clumsy and Grouchy were told to seek out Patrick. Patrick was, in fact, outside trying to open a manhole cover in the road as a way to get into the Opera House and Gargamel's secret lair. Suddenly, he was dazzled by the headlights of a car which was racing towards him! The car stopped suddenly – it was Victor.

"Grace told me where you'd be," the older man said. "I thought maybe you could use a hand?" Patrick was now only too happy for him to help.

© Peyo

Inside, Gargamel was still trying to get the formula from Smurfette. "Give it to him Smurfette!" Vexy said. "Then we can all be blue together."

"Hackus blue! Hackus blue!" burbled Hackus.

Smurfette paused thinking for a long time before she said: "The formula is a sacred gift entrusted to me. Sorry. I can't.." Gargamel exploded: "Can't???" he repeated. "I've given you everything! Kindness! Presents! A cake with no poison! It's been horrible! Now you will give me what I want – now – the formula!"

"No!" insisted Smurfette. Suddenly she looked to the Naughties. "What's happening to them?" Suddenly, Hackus fell over. Neither he nor Vexy looked very well. Gargamel grinned devilishly. _"Don't tell me you actually care for these creatures?" he asked. "How pathetic for you and how perfect for me! I thought you knew. Without the essence the Naughties cannot live."

Seeing Vexy wilt, Smurfette gave in. "Give them what you have! Take some from me!" she urged Gargamel.
"Why? What's the point?" said the wizard. "You won't give me the formula so I might as well just let them die. I can always make other Naughties." He shrugged.

Vexy looked into Smurfette's eyes with desperation. "Okay!, Smurfette said. "I'll give it to you. Feed them!" Gargamel slid over a pen and paper. "The formula first!" he insisted.

Just then, Papa broke through to a pipe from which he could see Smurfette. Sadly, the ongoing rush of the sewer water made it too loud for her to hear them. Vanity stretched his arm out through the grate. There was a pin there but it was just out of reach.

Meanwhile, Papa could not believe what he was seeing!
"… four hopeful thoughts, a dab of royal jelly, mimosa pollen and a drop of mink oil. And you must say one loving truth." Smurfette was giving up the formula to Gargamel! Gargamel put the ingredients into a nearby cauldron. Almost immediately long strands of blue smoke came out. The Naughties started to turn blue as they breathed them in. "Oh my Smurf!" shouted Gargamel excitedly. "It worked! The world is mine! I can now make Smurfs!" In the pipe, Papa watched in horror as Gargamel suddenly attempted to put a struggling Smurfette in the machine.

Meanwhile, Grouchy and Clumsy not only found Patrick and Victor. But by looking around the sewer system, they had also chanced upon an electricity generator. With any luck, switching off the generator could ruin Gargamel's plans.

Grouchy climbed onto Clumsy's shoulders and reached the lever. But which way to pull it? Negative or positive? "Try negative," shouted Patrick. "It might shut it off."

Grouchy thought for a moment. "No! You've got to be positive!" But when he pulled the lever, Grouchy was immediately electrocuted, blasted back and thrown into a bucket. The lights went out. Patrick, Victor and Clumsy all cheered: "Yes! We did it! We're heroes!" They said.

Grouchy was singed and back to his old self, however. "Why did I doubt negative?" he sighed.

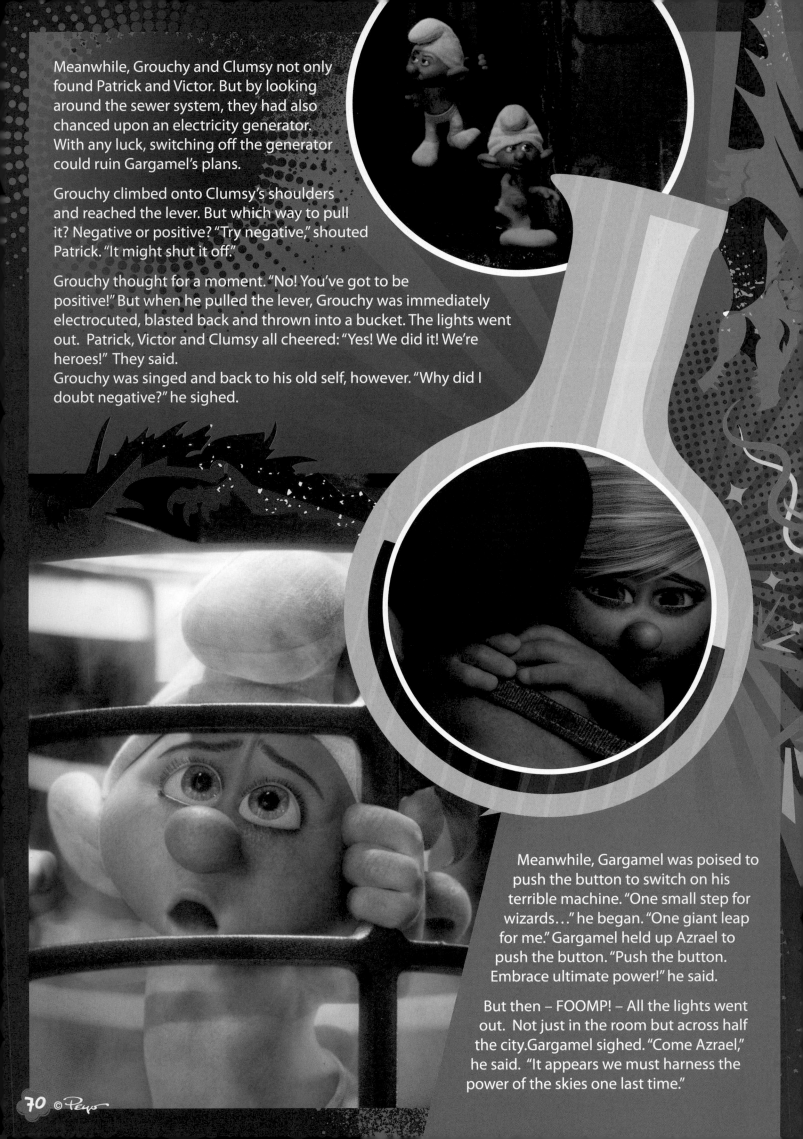

Meanwhile, Gargamel was poised to push the button to switch on his terrible machine. "One small step for wizards…" he began. "One giant leap for me." Gargamel held up Azrael to push the button. "Push the button. Embrace ultimate power!" he said.

But then – FOOMP! – All the lights went out. Not just in the room but across half the city.Gargamel sighed. "Come Azrael," he said. "It appears we must harness the power of the skies one last time."

© Peyo

Vanity finally pulled at the grate hard enough for it to come off. Vanity and Papa ran into the lair.

"Papa? Is that you? You came for me?" Smurfette said.

Of course we came for you," said Papa. "Was there ever a question?"

"Papa, I gave Gargamel the formula!" Smurfette admitted as Papa and Vanity freed her from the machine. "She saved our lives," said Vexy.

Papa Smurf looked at the three of them. "Don't apologise," he said. "A life is the most precious thing to protect. I'm proud of you." Just then, the lights came on. "Let's get the Smurf out of here!" "Wait," said Smurfette. "What about the Naughties?"

"What about them? They kidnapped you," said Grouchy. "They're Gargamel's."

"So was I," said Smurfette. "But Papa never gave up on me. And I'm not about to give up on them."

"And you thought you weren't a Smurf!" laughed Papa. "Unstrap them quickly!"

But suddenly Gargamel was there. He had harnessed lightning from the air and absorbed it into his wand. Before they knew it, the Smurfs were all tied to the Smurfalator.

"I want to be able to power…THIS!" The crazed wizard produced a huge wand carved in the shape of a large evil dragon. "I call her – Le Wanda. That's a joke because she's a wand," he explained. "That's funny. If you weren't all in terrible pain you'd be laughing."

Papa was struggling and had managed to loosen a bit of metal on one of the buckles which was holding him down. Meanwhile, Gargamel was filling up La Wanda directly from the essence tap.

"With this new power, I'm going to rule the world!" Gargamel declared. "My first official act will be to open a portal directly from the Smurf Village to my Smurfalator so that all the little Smurfs can be here forever!"

"You messed with the wrong Smoofs!" said a voice. It was Victor! He and Patrick were standing on top of the glass vat. "We're not Smoofs," corrected Patrick. "They're the Smoofs!"

"We're all Smoofs!" Vic yelled, raising the tire iron.

Just at that moment, Gargamel pointed La Wanda at them. But Papa managed to fling the piece of buckle at him, hitting La Wanda and causing it to misfire, hitting the vat. Instantly, the vat shattered causing an explosion of essence. The flow of essence hit the Smurfalator releasing the Naughties and the Smurfs and whooshing them away just as the shattered machine slammed into

Gargamel and the cat slamming them between it and the wall. The piece of paper with the secret formula written on sailed past before disappearing in a blue puff of smoke in front of Gargamel's eyes. The wave of blue energy carried the Smurfs through the sewers, leaving a trail of flowers in its wake before blasting the Smurfs onto the pavement outside. The whole street was now awash with a sea of Smurfy blue energy.

"We did it!" shouted Patrick rushing to Grace as he spotted her nearby.
Smurfette helped Vexy up too – they looked down at their reflection in a puddle. Vexy was now lovely and blue.
"Now that's the real you!" Smurfette said. They both laughed. Smurfette introduced Vexy to Grace. "This is my sister!" she said. Vexy grew teary eyed. "Is this what happy feels like?" she asked.

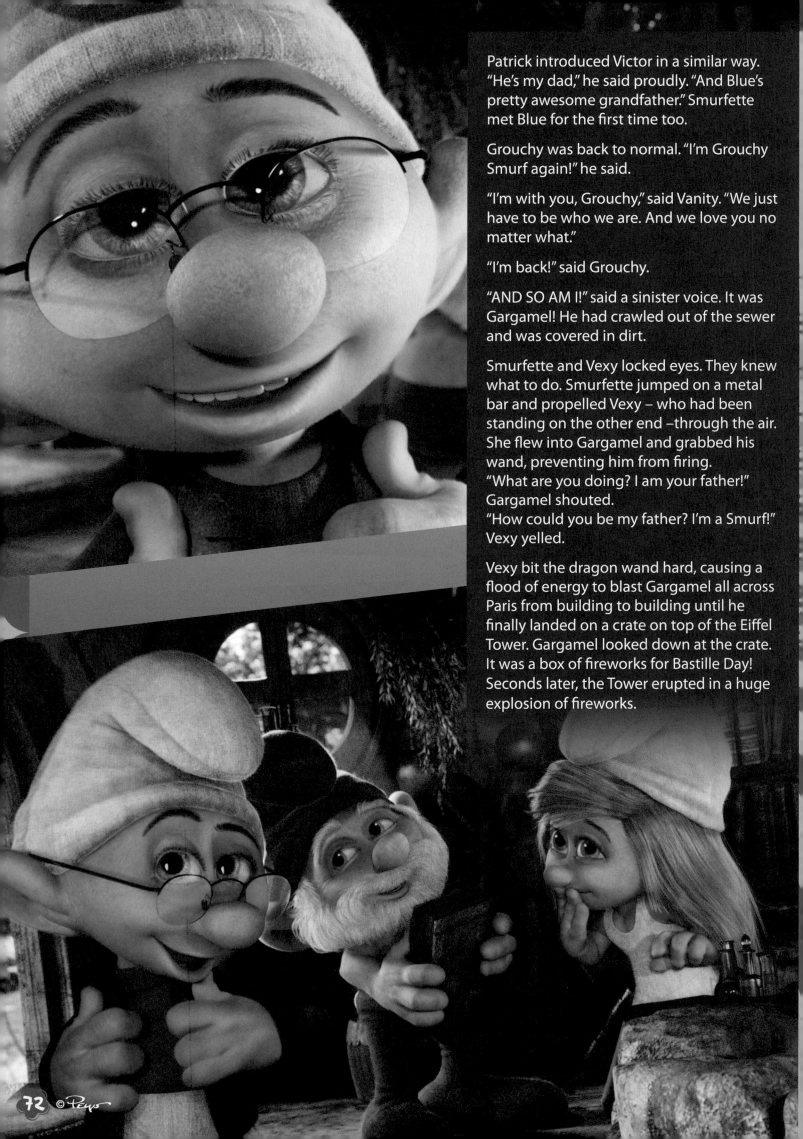

Patrick introduced Victor in a similar way. "He's my dad," he said proudly. "And Blue's pretty awesome grandfather." Smurfette met Blue for the first time too.

Grouchy was back to normal. "I'm Grouchy Smurf again!" he said.

"I'm with you, Grouchy," said Vanity. "We just have to be who we are. And we love you no matter what."

"I'm back!" said Grouchy.

"AND SO AM I!" said a sinister voice. It was Gargamel! He had crawled out of the sewer and was covered in dirt.

Smurfette and Vexy locked eyes. They knew what to do. Smurfette jumped on a metal bar and propelled Vexy – who had been standing on the other end –through the air. She flew into Gargamel and grabbed his wand, preventing him from firing.
"What are you doing? I am your father!" Gargamel shouted.
"How could you be my father? I'm a Smurf!" Vexy yelled.

Vexy bit the dragon wand hard, causing a flood of energy to blast Gargamel all across Paris from building to building until he finally landed on a crate on top of the Eiffel Tower. Gargamel looked down at the crate. It was a box of fireworks for Bastille Day! Seconds later, the Tower erupted in a huge explosion of fireworks.

© Peyo

All was well until Papa noticed they only had five crystals left and they needed seven. Smurfette quickly magicked up some more.

"Wow Smurfette!" said Grace. "You're pretty good with that wand."

"It's sort of in my blood, which used to freak me out," said Smurfette looking at Papa. "But as someone wonderful once told me, it doesn't matter where you came from. What matters is what you choose to be."

Back at the Smurf Village, night had fallen. The Smurfs were gathered in the centre when there was a POP, POP, POP, POP, POP! The Smurfs ran up the hill and soon saw Papa.

"Papa! You got Smurfette!" said Clever. "And some more Smurfs! Everyone – this is Vexy!" said Smurfette.

Everyone froze but Hefty liked her. A lot. "Holy Smurfoli! Do they all look like her?"

Vexy was surprised too. "Wow. All these boys!"

"And just two girls…" said Smurfette.

"What do you mean? Hackus is a girl," said Vexy. Hackus was surprised. "Hackus is girl?" Hackus immediately chased after Hefty and attempted to hug him.

"Wait Hackus! I was kidding!" shouted Vexy. "Hackus don't care. Hackus love family!"

A huge party was held for Smurfette's birthday. It was slightly late but nobody really minded. And a great time was had by all.

The End

Brainy's

CHALLENGE PART 3

GO FOR IT!

1 WHICH TYPE OF BIRD DOES NOT APPEAR IN THE STORY?

- A An eagle.
- B A stork.
- C A duck.

2 WHICH CHARACTER DOES NOT CELEBRATE A BIRTHDAY DURING THIS ADVENTURE?

- A Blue.
- B Patrick.
- C Smurfette.

3 WHO IS THE ONLY SMURF NOT TO WEAR A WHITE HAT?

- A Papa Smurf.
- B Smurfette.
- C Vanity.

4 WHICH OF THESE IS NOT A SMURF?

- A Odile.
- B Hefty.
- C Jokey.

5 HACKUS ACCIDENTALLY JUMPS ON WHAT?

- A A trolley.
- B A fashion model.
- C Gargamel.

6 GARGAMEL ENDS UP BEING BLOWN OFF THE TOP OF WHICH BUILDING?

- A The Eiffel Tower.
- B The Mini Statue of Liberty.
- C Big Ben.

SO, HAVE YOU DONE ALL OF BRAINY'S CHALLENGES? DID YOU KEEP A RECORD OF YOUR FINAL SCORE?

ANSWERS ON PAGE 77

HOW DID YOU DO?

USE THIS HANDY GUIDE TO SEE HOW SMURFTASTIC YOU ARE?

CAN YOU BEAT BRAINY AT HIS OWN GAME? HERE'S YOUR LAST CHANCE TO TRY BRAINY'S CHALLENGE.

TOT UP YOUR FINAL SCORES FROM THIS AND THE OTHER TWO BRAINY'S CHALLENGES IN THE BOOK AND THEN ADD UP YOUR TOTAL TO FIND OUT HOW SMURFTASTIC YOU ARE. BELOW!

7 WHICH SMURF IS THE VILLAGE CHIEF?

- A Smurfette.
- B Vanity.
- C Papa Smurf.

8 WHO BECOMES SMURFETTE'S NEW SISTER?

- A Vexy.
- B Grace.
- C Odile.

9 WHAT IS GARGAMEL'S JOB?

- A Doctor.
- B Musician.
- C Magician.

10 WHICH SMURF WEARS GLASSES?

- A Brainy.
- B Vanity.
- C Clumsy.

11 WHICH SMURF TALKS FAR TOO MUCH?

- A Smurfette.
- B Clumsy.
- C Narrator Smurf.

12 WHO DOES THE GIANT AZRAEL VERY NEARLY EAT?

- A Patrick.
- B Victor.
- C Gargamel.

Smurf zactly!

IF YOU SCORED: 0–12 OH DEAR! YOU CERTAINLY HAVE SOME WAY TO GO IN LEARNING ABOUT SMURFS! BUT NEVER MIND: YOU ARE FREE TO COMPLETE BRAINY'S CHALLENGES AS MANY TIMES AS YOU LIKE. BETTER LUCK NEXT TIME!

IF YOU SCORED: 13–24 NOT BAD AT ALL! THERE'S STILL PLENTY OF ROOM FOR IMPROVEMENT BUT YOU STILL KNOW MORE THAN MOST PEOPLE ABOUT THE SMURFING WORLD.

IF YOU SCORED: 25–36 OH WOW! ARE YOU ACTUALLY A SMURF YOURSELF? YOU ARE SO SMURFTASTIC. IT IS SURPRISING YOU ARE NOT ACTUALLY BLUE! AND GUESS WHAT? BRAINY IS ANNOYED BECAUSE EVEN THOUGH HE WROTE THE CHALLENGE, YOU ACTUALLY DID BETTER THAN HIM! WELL DONE!

SMURFETTE'S Dot TO Dot PUZZLE

WHAT DOES SMURFETTE LIKE MOST ABOUT BIRTHDAYS! JOIN THE DOTS AND FIND OUT!

ANSWERS

PG 22 PAPA'S PARIS PUZZLER

PATRICK DOES NOT APPEAR. HE WAS BACK AT THE HOTEL ALL ALONG!)

PG 23 HELP SMURFETTE ESCAPE!

PG 24 BRAINY'S CHALLENGE – PT1

1: IT'S SMURFETTE'S BIRTHDAY PARTY. 2: THE NAUGHTIES, VEXY AND HACKUS. 3: SHE IS SCARED OF GARGAMEL BUT IS MAINLY WORRIED THAT SHE MAY GROW UP TO BE LIKE HIM. 4: HE IS THE HOST OF A FAMOUS MAGIC SHOW WHICH TOURS AROUND THE WORLD. 5: HE DECIDES TO BE LESS GRUMPY AND MORE POSITIVE. 6: A DUCK. 7: PATRICK'S STEP-FATHER. 8: PARIS. 9: SOME STORKS. 10: WANDA. 11: HE INTENDS TO USE THE EIFFEL TOWER AS A GIANT TRANSMITTER. 12: SHE IS UNSURE AS TO WHETHER SHE IS A PROPER SMURF OR GARGAMEL'S DAUGHTER.

PG 26 JOIN THE DOTS

CLUMSY.

PG 28 GARGAMEL'S MAGICAL MYSTERY

IVY TAN = VANITY, BIN RAY = BRAINY
CHORGUY = GROUCHY.
WEARING SCOWL = GRACE WINSLOW
FARMS RUN TAR OR = NARRATOR SMURF

PG 29 IN THE SHADOWS

THIS IS THE SILHOUETTE OF PAPA SMURF.

PG 38 VANITY'S MYSTERY MIRROR

NUMBER 3.

PG 39 LOOK WHO'S TALKING?

PG 42 BRAINY'S CHALLENGE – PT2

1: HEFTY. 2: BLUE. 3: HE NEEDS SMURF ESSENCE TO FUEL HIS MAGIC TRICKS AND WORK TOWARDS TAKING OVER THE WORLD. 4: A SWEET SHOP. 5: CLUMSY. 6: THEY ARE BUSY PLANNING HER SURPRISE PARTY. 7: CANADA. 8: PATRICK'S CHILDHOOD COMPANION: A PARROT. 9: FOR GIVING GARGAMEL THE FORMULA. 10: VICTOR. 11: SISTER AND BROTHER. 12: A FERRIS WHEEL.

PG 46 HIDE & SEEK

PG 49 BRAINY'S MATHS PUZZLER

THE NUMBER OF NAUGHTIES = 2
THE NUMBER OF SMURFS WHO GO TO PARIS TO RESCUE SMURFETTE = 4
(PAPA, VANITY, CLUMSY & GROUCHY)
THE AGE OF BLUE ON HIS BIRTHDAY = 2
THE NUMBER OF STORKS FLOWN ON = 3
ANSWER IS 7!

PG 60 CLOSE-UPS!

1: VEXY. 2: BRAINY. 3: HEFTY.
4: SMURFETTE. 5: GROUCHY.
6: HACKUS. 7: PAPA SMURF

PG 63 HELP SMURFETTE REMEMBER

PG 64 HEFTY'S TRUE OR FALSE QUIZ

1: TRUE. 2: FALSE. 3: FALSE. 4: TRUE.
5: FALSE. 6: TRUE (FRANCE IS IN EUROPE).
7: FALSE (PAPA SMURF IS). 8: FALSE.
9: FALSE. 10: TRUE

PG 65 CLUMSY'S MIX UP

FAR UP MAPS = PAPA SMURF
FEET STRUM = SMURFETTE
NITPICK SLOW WAR = PATRICK WINSLOW
OILED = ODILE
ZEALAR = AZRAEL

PG 74 BRAINY'S CHALLENGE – PT3

1: AN EAGLE. 2: PATRICK. 3: PAPA SMURF.
4: ODILE. 5: A FASHION MODEL.
6: THE EIFFEL TOWER. 7: PAPA SMURF.
8: VEXY. 9: MAGICIAN. 10: BRAINY.
11: NARRATOR SMURF. 12: PATRICK.

PG 76 SMURFETTE'S DOT TO DOT

BIRTHDAY CAKE.

The Smurfs 2 Annual 2014

Visit **Pedigreebooks.com** to find out more on this year's **The Smurfs 2 Annual**, scan with your mobile device to learn more.

Visit www.pedigreebooks.com

Pedigree Books, Beech Hill House, Walnut Gardens, Exeter EX4 4DH